CHRISTMAS AT EAGLE POND

Books by Donald Hall

Prose

CHRISTMAS AT EAGLE POND

Donald Hall

Godine
BOSTON

Published in 2018 by
Godine
www.godine.com

First published by Houghton Mifflin Harcourt in 2012

Library of Congress Cataloging-in-Publication Data
Names: Hall, Donald, 1928–2018 author.
Title: Christmas at Eagle Pond / Donald Hall.
Description: Jaffrey, New Hampshire : David R. Godine, Publisher, 2017.
Identifiers: LCCN 2017041692 | ISBN 9781567926095 (softcover : acid-free
paper) Subjects: LCSH: Farm life--Fiction. | Christmas stories. |
GSAFD: Autobiographical fiction.
Classification: LCC PS3515.A3152 C48 2017 | DDC 813/.54--dc23
LC record available at https://lccn.loc.gov/2017041692

Book design by Melissa Lotfy
Illustrations by Mary Azarian

THIRD PRINTING, 2021
Printed in the United States of America

For Alison Granucci

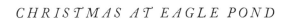

CHRISTMAS AT EAGLE POND

SUNDAY

O N THE WINTER SOLSTICE of 1940, the dark-est day, I rode a train into central New Hampshire. I was twelve and traveled for Christmas to my grandparents' Eagle Pond Farm, where I spent summers haying with my grandfather. The Boston and Maine passenger train was a puffing steam engine followed by a coal car, a mail car, and a coach barely populated. We slowed and stopped in West Andover, at the tiny depot called Gale, and the conduc-tor — in the summer he wore a handkerchief tucked between his collar and his neck — set down the yellow step for me to descend with my suitcase. Dimly in the darkness, I saw what

I looked for: my grandfather Wesley Wells with his horse and buggy, Gramp whispering into Riley's ear because the clatter of the train made him skittery.

We said, "Gramp!" "Donnie!" and hugged. We stuffed my suitcase behind the buggy's seat. My grandfather had always before picked me up in the high light of June. This Sunday it was wholly dark at six P.M., with scrappy snow on the ground. I saw that Gramp had hung oil lamps at the front and back of the buggy, and now — having snuffed them out to save kerosene as he waited for my train — he lit them again with a wooden kitchen match. We climbed into the seat and set out for the farm. There were few cars on the road, but we needed to be visible as we rattled down Route 4 with wheels in the gutter. Two Model A's pulled around us. We passed the glacial boulder looming through the darkness at the side of the road. Riley shied at it, although he had passed it ten thousand times.

After we spoke encouraging words about my mother's operation, we hardly talked; we were both too excited. Ahead I watched for the lights of Eagle Pond Farm, and soon I saw not only the porch light but through the window a lighted Christmas tree.

. . .

My parents and I lived in Hamden, Connecticut, a suburb of New Haven. I was a single child, like so many during the Depression. My mother's operation had been successful — she would recover fully — but medical habits were different in those days, and my mother remained in the hospital ten days. Soon she would be home, in bed upstairs; there would be little Christmas in Hamden on December 25. For many years I had asked my parents if we could drive north to the farm for Christmas, because I wanted to see it in winter, and because my mother had entertained me with her girlhood memories of Christmas there. This year they let me go by myself. It was my biggest present.

My father drove me to the New Haven railroad station — a great cathedral, high-ceilinged over rows of benches, one wall grated with ticket stalls. We bought my ticket to Boston, and my father nervously put me and my suitcase on the streamliner, its engine shaped like a bullet wearing skirts. I took a window seat as the train puffed through the railway yards past empty passenger cars and unloaded freight trains. We chugged by rows of houses beside the noisy tracks and emerged into a countryside bordered by Long Island Sound. Between the train and the water hovered the remains of a derelict trolley line that once took passengers, with many stops and transfers, from Boston down the coast to New Haven. Over the marshes, the broken line swooped on great wooden trestles, dangling tracks where a thousand seagulls perched.

The train stopped in New London, Westerly, Kingston, Providence, Back Bay, and finally pulled into Boston's enormous South Station. My aunt Nan, youngest of three Eagle Pond sisters, was waiting for me as I stepped off the streamliner. She was working in a Boston bookstore while her husband did a stint in the Coast Guard. My parents had been relieved that she could lead me across Boston, although I could have done it myself. I felt babied. A yellow cab took us to the smaller and older North Station, where the Boston and Maine dispatched trains north to Maine, New Hampshire, and Vermont. I bought my ticket and waited an hour talking with my aunt before departure. We hugged and said goodbye, and I climbed into the little train we called the Peanut. There were two passenger cars, and I boarded the front one because the second would be dropped off at the big city of Manchester, New Hampshire. The Peanut went all the way to White River Junction in Vermont, stopping at a dozen depots on the way, and returned the morning after. Now it passed through the populous area north of Boston, through Lowell and Lawrence and into farming country. For the first time I looked at snow on hayfields, and on barns that sheltered Holstein cattle. Approaching Manchester I watched as houses displaced fields. We dropped the second car and headed toward Concord, the state capital, where a railway station rose on the alluvial plain of the Merrimack River. Then the Peanut stopped every few miles — Penacook, Boscawen, past farmland into the market town of Franklin. We stopped at the East Andover depot named Halcyon, three miles later Andover, two miles later Potter Place, two miles later West Andover, where my grandfather waited at its depot called Gale. The stations were close together because, not so long in the past, farmers carted their milk by oxen to the railroad's morning milk car, on its way to Boston and H. P. Hood. These days, a truck picked up the cans at Eagle Pond Farm.

We pulled into the U-shaped driveway, my grandmother smiling in the kitchen door wearing a cardigan over her print dress and apron. While my grandfather backed the buggy into the carriage shed, detached Riley, and led him to his stall, my grandmother Kate held me close. I followed her into the kitchen, warm from the range's fire. Gramp had finished his chores and supper before picking me up, and now he joined us as Gram served me baked beans with brown bread. I was mopping up the last of the beans when the telephone rang twice, which on our party line meant that the call was for us. Central told Gram that it was person-to-person for Donnie Hall, which didn't surprise anybody. Gram gave me the phone, and I heard my mother's frail voice from the hospital bed. I told her I was fine, how was she? She was feeling stronger, she said, and handed the phone to my father. He repeated that my mother felt better. "By the time you get back," he said, "her doctor says she'll be home. Soon she'll be downstairs sitting up."

The cows already milked, now Gramp shut up the chickens, and we sat in the living room, warmed by the Glenwood stove. My grandfather spoke vigorously of "Franklin Delano Roosevelt" — Gramp sounded like a Fourth of July orator — and his reelection last month, the first third term for an American president. Gramp was the world's most enthusiastic Democrat; possibly he was New Hampshire's only Democrat. His father had been a Copperhead, and brought up his children to despise Lincoln's party, although he fought in the Civil War to march with his neighbors. Gramp's voice quieted down as we spoke together of the

war in Europe, and how we would inevitably join it — despite the crazies at America First yelling about staying out. We talked until we turned on the radio that took up a corner of the room. On weekdays in summer evenings, we listened to Gabriel Heatter's booming dramatic voice, as plump as a pumpkin, when he gave his nine o'clock fifteen minutes of news. Today was Sunday and we heard an ordinary voice. The Luftwaffe's incendiaries burned London; Piccadilly was in flames. When the news ended it was time for bed. My grandmother drank her cheese glass of warm Moxie; my grandfather slurped his bread and milk. Gram took the kettle from the range and filled hot-water bottles. I walked through their icy bedroom to mine, even icier, and stuffed my hot-water bottle under the sheets to warm my feet. Crawling beneath the covers I shivered a moment, but the quilts were thick, my feet almost too hot, and soon I fell asleep in my familiar goosefeather bed at the house I loved most in the world.

MONDAY

A T SIX IN THE MORNING, I woke for a moment to hear my grandparents stirring in the room beside me. From my summers I knew what would happen while I fell back asleep. Gramp and Gram walked past the cold stove in the living room to the cold range in the kitchen. We kept a box of wood beside it. (When I was at the farm, everything was "we" and "our.") Gram lifted the iron lid over the firebox, and Gramp set kindling and small logs inside. He brought from the toolshed a tin can brimmed with kerosene, which he poured over the nest of firewood. Scratching a match against the stove, he hurled it onto the soaked wood, and immediately a blaze leapt high and my grandmother covered it with the lid. As the fire rumbled, the range began to warm. Gram filled a silvery percolator with water and coffee — and filled it again all day, so that coffee as strong as Charles Atlas kept warm on the stove. Soon I heard the winter Glenwood in the living room, loaded with logs and doused with kerosene, begin to heat the big room. On hooks behind the stove my clothes warmed up.

At half past six Gram rapped on my bedroom door. "Coffee's ready." I clutched my goosefeather warmth around me for a last moment, then dashed in my pajamas to stand beside the Glenwood, fierce with its draft open. I dressed in wool socks, wool pants, wool shirt, and pulled on a wool sweater. I sat in the kitchen with a cup of coffee, looking forward to the day. I knew that tonight would be the annual Christmas party at church. Through the window I saw Gramp climbing to the barn to milk the cattle, where he would be kept tolerably warm by Holstein bodies on each side. The morning was the twenty-third, dawn's light still faint. Probably he would hook a lantern to the wall of the tie-up behind him. I would join him soon.

As I stretched myself in the warmth, my grandmother braided her long hair at the kitchen window, beside her caged canary always called Christopher. She looked out the window toward Kearsarge, just visible, and said, "Mountain's real pretty today," as she said almost every morning. When she said, "Can't see the mountain too good today," it meant a storm was on the way. I stepped onto the porch, chilly as it was, to glance at the white landscape which I adored green in summer. In the middle of the lawn rose a great maple, shade for the porch in July, now naked and stark against the lightening sky. When I was five or six, another maple rose beside it. My grandfather made a swing for me, hooking a wooden pole between branches from each tree, with ropes hanging from the pole and a board for a seat. The hurricane of 1938 knocked down the older maple.

Tall elms rose on both sides of Route 4. Farther away Mount Kearsarge loomed as it did in the kitchen window, deity of the sandy lowlands. It was only about three thousand feet high, what in the West would be considered a foothill, but here it seemed huge. I could see the light blinking on its watchtower. Kearsarge was conical, like a spent volcano, and it lifted its snow-covered trees to a flat patch of bare rock, gradually turning bright with snow as the rising sun caught the mountain. Each summer I climbed Kearsarge. My mother and her sisters climbed it when they were girls, my grandmother Kate before them, and I'm sure all my ancestors at Eagle Pond Farm.

To my left, beside the barn, rose the slopes of Ragged Mountain, a low hill eight miles long that ranged from Andover to Danbury. When it turned green, it would become pasture for the cattle of our farm. In the other direction, across the road, lay seven flat acres where we grew the year's food, where I was accustomed to look not at snow but at green plants. Beyond the beans and root vegetables would rise rows of sweet corn, then an acre of field corn, which was chopped into ensilage, and which the cows ate all winter. Today, looking west past the flat and trackless white, past the railroad tracks, I could make out snow covering Eagle Pond. (In summer, through the leaves of oak and maple, I saw the sparkle of its water.) As I stood in landscape-ecstasy, my grandmother's voice interrupted me. "Eggs are ready. Come inside, you'll catch your death."

When I had eaten breakfast, I put on galoshes, winter coat, and mittens that Gram had knitted for me last Christmas. I trudged uphill to the barn. The cattle, six Holsteins and one Jersey, were chained in a row that occupied about a quarter of the big barn, on the side that backed up to Ragged Mountain. We called it the tie-up. Gramp sat between cows on an old armchair with its legs cut off, pulling on Holstein teats with his cold bare hands as milk foamed in the bucket. "Donnie!" he called. I hugged his shoulders where he sat. I loved to watch him milk, summer and now winter, as I squatted on a three-legged stool and his fingers stripped the udders clean. It was while Gramp milked — or on our summer rides home in the hayrack — that he spoke his pieces to entertain me. As a boy he had memorized poems to recite at the gatherings of the South Danbury Oratorical and Debating Society. Before radio, before television, these meetings were entertainment for young people from the countryside. Twice a month they gathered at night in a schoolhouse. Before the debate, a girl might play the piano, another sing a song, and the young Wesley Wells would speak his rhymed stories, either funny or dramatic. He remembered dozens, and every year told me new ones he had recalled when I was away. This morning he spoke two of my favorites, "Lawyer Blue" and "An Orphan Lad from Boston." Reciting, he made the gestures he learned from nineteenth-century oratorical books, where children were taught facial expressions to accompany texts: astonishment, grief, disdain, approval. I loved his recitations as much as I loved the country stories he told me out of memory. The culture of these hills and pastures perpetuated itself in storytelling. Whenever the older generation gathered, often on Sunday afternoons — the only hours free of work — story followed story. Younger people sat silent, appearing dumb or passive, but when they themselves were older, they became the storytellers.

When he had finished filling a pail of milk, Gramp poured it into a big milkcan topped with a paper filter. In summer spiders and flies flew everywhere; in winter hay chaff floated in the air. Once a year Gramp scraped the walls of the tie-up and applied a fresh coat of whitewash, and once a year the agricultural inspector paid a visit.

As Gramp moved from cow to cow, I left the tie-up to look into the empty main floor of the barn. One electric bulb, high up, gave out a little light. I walked to Riley in his stall and stroked his jaws. He was an old horse now; my mother remembered him from twenty years ago. From his stall, an open window looked on Route 4, and when he wasn't working he stuck his head out watching the traffic. Past Riley there were empty stalls for two oxen — New Hampshire farms once prospered — which used to do the heaviest work, pulling wood down the mountain or blocks of ice from Eagle Pond. In the oxen's vacant stall Gramp had stowed a fancy, cobwebby sleigh, its wooden arms sticking out onto the barn floor as if it were ready to go. Gramp visited me from the tie-up, and stretched as I gazed. "Haven't used that sleigh for fifteen years," he said, "ever since they started plowing Route 4." It was a handsome wooden sculpture, its front curving gracefully from its lowest point up to the seat. The wood must have been steamed a long time to bend so extravagantly. Just beyond the ox stall, toward the chained cattle, were bins of grain, oats, and meal for the animals. The bins were wooden, smooth with age and splendid with plenty, unlike the vacancy of the stalls. Gramp scooped oats for Riley, then went back to the tie-up to milk his last cows.

The barn's main floor was where Riley pulled the summer hayrack. In August's heat we pitched hay up to vast lofts on the second and third levels. I was not sweating today. Shivering, I returned to Gramp and the cows. When he was done milking, this morning and every morning, he lifted the two milkcans onto a wheelbarrow, handmade and painted farmhouse green, to roll them downhill and set them on a platform where the truck would pick them up. He knew when the truck came; milk didn't freeze in the winter or spoil in the summer.

More chores followed milking. It was time for the cattle

to drink from their watering trough. First my grandfather broke through the lid of ice that formed overnight, then one by one he unchained his cows; they knew where to go. While they drank, Gramp walked back into the main floor and climbed a homemade ladder — two split rails, maybe three inches wide, dowels driven into them for rungs — up to a loft and pushed summer's hay down to feed the cows. We topped off the dry grass with sweet ensilage from the indoor silo. When the cattle walked back to their stalls from their long drink of water, they chewed their breakfast-lunch-dinner. We linked chains around their necks and cleaned behind them, lifting a board in the floor, hinged with leather straps, so we could scrape cowflops onto the heap under the barn. (Next to that pile stood the honey wagon, which Gramp used when he spread manure for garden and field corn.) After Gramp hauled Riley a pail of water, we crossed the road to the sheep barn, letting the sheep loose to drink from another trough. We forked them the brambly hay that only they would eat.

We watched my grandmother leave the hen yard, her apron under her winter coat bulging with a dozen eggs or more, our winter food crop. Some we ate for breakfast, some went into baking, and the rest we traded with Henry

Powers, who ran the tiny grocery store near Gale. We traded for salt and coffee, which were not New Hampshire crops. Mostly we ate what we grew. Our sweetness came from honey and maple syrup, and we brewed vinegar from cider stored in rootcellar barrels. For our meat, we ate setting hens, so tough that it took two hours' boiling to soften them for chicken fricassee. We ate deermeat — venison in Connecticut — when neighbors in fall shot a buck. A grubby year-round butcher drove to the farm once a week, selling bad joints of meat for a dollar or so. Our bread was homemade, spread with home-churned butter. Churning was one of my grandmother's chores, which were as heavy as my grandfather's. Monday washing, Tuesday ironing, Wednesday baking . . . and every day the chickens, every day the darning, knitting, and tatting. Once a year she made soap.

This morning Gramp, as on other December and January days, undertook his winter work of chopping wood on Ragged. However cold it was today, we needed wood for next year. Gram fixed his midday dinner — butter-and-jelly sandwiches in wax paper along with blueberry muffins baked last Wednesday — and tucked it into a pail with a thermos of coffee. He set off up-mountain carrying his dinner in a mittened hand, the other gripping the handle of a shiny ax slung over his shoulder. The only task I ever heard him complain about was winter's harvest of trees. The cold sky lightened as he climbed, wearing boots over three pairs of wool socks. He cut down old trees, preferably ash, trimmed off small branches, then chopped the trunks into four-foot lengths. Gram worried — a tree falling on him, the ax cutting him — but the house required ten cords a year, not only for winter, but for summer's cooking and canning.

Winter chores continued in February, when the ice was two feet thick on Eagle Pond. He sliced next summer's coolness from the frozen water, to keep the August milk from spoiling overnight. With a saw he cut solid oblongs and stored them under sawdust in the icehouse. (Last summer I went with him as Riley pulled an empty cart up New Canada Road to a mill that had accumulated foothills of sawdust. They let us take it for nothing, clearing away their debris.) When February turned into March, his daily tasks became easier. For maple sugaring, he tapped the trees uphill behind the sap house, and sap dripped into buckets, which he emptied into pails that he carried downhill, great vessels dangling at each end of a yoke that lay across his shoulders. Boiling sap into syrup, the fire had to burn twenty-four hours a day under the great steel tray. Our eccentric cousin

Freeman Morrison — whom I saw sickly last summer, who died just a month ago — liked to sleep by day and work by night. He pushed small trees foot by foot into the perpetual fire.

With Gramp up-mountain, I helped Gram empty ash from the stoves, shaking them out over snow for safety's sake. I followed her to the henhouse, scattering for the chickens our remains from supper and breakfast. My grandmother made beds, then gathered clothes for washing. She pushed the washer into the kitchen, its mangle on its side, filled it with hot water, and started Monday's work, while I read until lunch.

At noon we ate fried Spam, and beets from the rootcellar doused with vinegar from the cruet. Gram hung washed clothes from wooden wands that spread above the range, and put sheets to freeze-dry on a porch clothesline. Then she said we would make popcorn balls to hang on the church tree at the party tonight, for the children to take home if they didn't eat them right away. Gram went downstairs and brought up a quart of my grandfather's maple syrup, which she poured into a saucepan on the range. It began to bubble. Over the firebox she placed a big kettle, melted lard, and poured in popcorn kernels. With a lid she covered the kettle. Soon I heard soft explosions inside, which gradually slowed down and stopped. She removed the kettle from the heat and checked out the bubbly syrup. When it turned thick, we cleared the worn, flowered oilcloth on the set tubs, spread wax paper, and poured out the lukewarm popcorn. She carried the saucepan of condensed syrup from stove to oilcloth and dribbled maple glue over the pile. We molded sticky sweet balls, the size of baseballs, a messy and hilarious business. By the time we had constructed thirty or more, our hands were as sticky as our confections, which we left to dry. Gram set a wash pan in the sink, ran faucet water, and warmed it with a ladle of water from the reservoir at the end of the range. With a chunk of her soap and dishrags we cleaned our hands. After an hour the balls were still sticky as we dropped each one in a little bag of red mesh, with a loop, which we would dangle from the church tree.

Just then my aunt Caroline drove into the yard, home for Christmas from Reading, Massachusetts, where she taught English in high school. Caroline was a year younger than my mother, my literary aunt who took me walking when I was little and told me stories about a Greek sailor who outsmarted a one-eyed giant. She arrived in her black

Chevrolet when it was dark and we had lit the tree. We hugged and chatted until she carried her suitcase to a freezing upstairs bedroom. When she came down she set her wrapped packages under the tree, then brought from her car a plate of Christmas cookies, sprinkled with red and green sparkling sugar. We each had a cookie, even if supper was near.

Gramp had come down from the mountain in early darkness to milk the cows. The Christmas party would begin at seven, and we ate supper at six, then drove two miles in Caroline's car to park at the South Danbury Church among the Model A's and at least one Model T. A few horses, buggies behind them, neighed in the horse shed that tilted by the church. When my mother was a girl, the shed filled up with sleighs, not buggies. Before Route 4 was paved and plowed for automobiles, my grandfather paid his town taxes by smoothing the snow, flattening it down for sleighs between our house in Wilmot and the Danbury line. His old snow roller, a steamroller without steam, stood under a shed beside the chicken yard, as useless now as the sleigh in the cow barn.

The church, normally spare, was loudly Protestant. There were no pictures on the walls, not even a cross (which would have been idolatrous), only a wooden clock, wound on Sunday, that told the time for a whole week with nobody watching. In winter the church was kept warm by two wood-stoves that burned at the back, their stovepipes traversing the ceiling toward chimneys up front. The Ordways and the Fifields, who lived by the church, hauled the wood, set the fires, and tended them.

My great-uncle Luther, Gram's elder brother, was minister, and puttered around the altar. Uncle Lu was bent, with sparse hair and a white mustache. Born in 1856, he told me stories from the middle of the last century. For decades he had served parishes elsewhere in New England, returning to his birthplace when he retired. He kept a little cottage called Sabine down the road — Aunt Alice had died, the children grown up — but when he felt poorly he used a bedroom upstairs at the farm. Gram called it the Best Room; ministers deserved the best, and at dinner Luther was served first and started eating right away. In the Best Room, Luther slept in the bed he'd brought with him when he retired, a big black construction with a footboard and a tall headboard painted with gold designs like Egyptian hieroglyphs. I found the painted bed mysterious. Luther never spoke about the symbols and bright curlicues, but

his bed was clearly dear to him. Luther also owned an el-
derly Studebaker; it was scary to ride with him. Taking a
left-hand turn, he swerved into the left lane to save gas and
rubber.

Walking inside, I was dazzled by the church's transfor-
mation, from the plain place of summer Sundays, by Christmas wreaths and the great tree. This morning the Phelps
family had set up the tree in a corner. The Christmas Party
Committee had strung the lights, with a flickering star on
top, and added ornaments and icicles. My grandmother and
I hung our popcorn balls, and Gram took her place at the
organ. I sat beside Gramp in the pew that Gram's father had
bought in 1866. My grandmother, who became regular or-
ganist when she was thirteen, pumped a few practice chords.
I looked around me and saw Robert, a boy my age, with his
mother and father, Huldah and John. I saw my cousin Edna
with her husband Ansel and their little boy Forrest, named
after a Civil War general like all the neighborhood Grants
and Shermans. I saw Curriers, Sanborns, Fifields, Welles,
Powerses, Whittemores, Ordways, Fords, and Phelpses.
These were the people who had never moved away, who
stayed home while their brothers and sisters departed.
From my summers I knew everyone, tonight disguised by

coats and scarves. Underneath, everyone had dressed as if for a Sunday service, my grandfather in a brown suit that had been my father's, my grandmother in the Sunday dress she had sewn at her Singer. I wore a jacket and a necktie, as twelve-year-old boys did in 1940. For the Christmas party the altar was moved to the side, and in the center of its platform rested a small wooden cradle. By six forty-five the pews were full, because we were to start at seven. In New Hampshire time, seven o'clock meant six forty-five, because everybody was early for everything. In Connecticut, if my parents wanted friends to come for dinner at eight, they asked them for seven-thirty.

An eager audience waited for the Sunday school children to speak their pieces. There were parents, grandparents, aunts and uncles, older siblings, former Sunday schoolers, even cousins who drove from distances as great as ten miles. Conspicuous in the front row sat the Sunday school children themselves, dressed in their best, the girls with ribbons, the boys with slicked hair. There were three-year-olds who couldn't keep quiet, alongside eight-year-olds of severe dignity. When Uncle Luther wearing his black suit ascended the platform, everyone hushed to hear his prayer. We sang "We Three Kings of Orient Are."

One of the elder Sunday schoolers stood, turned to face the pews, and said the Lord's Prayer — correctly, rapidly, and inaudibly. Sitting next to the children was Pamela Sanborn, chief Sunday school teacher, who had rehearsed them for weeks, and who watched her pupils with anxiety. She turned toward the crowd and announced, "Now Hester will play the piano." Across the platform from the organ was the venerable instrument, never tuned, where Hester sat and thumped "It Came upon a Midnight Clear."

As I watched, I thought of my mother's memories. It was the same building, the same families, with many of the same rituals — but in my mother's time the Christmas party punctuated the whole year. There were always the popcorn balls, but her church — she was born in 1903 — differed considerably from 1940's. In her childhood, the crowded Sunday services were two hours in the morning and two in the afternoon. At the church party back then, parishioners gave family members all their Christmas presents. My mother and her sisters unwrapped their two annual surprises, for each a doll with a china head, and for each a new storybook. Their mother acquired these gifts with coupons from the Great Atlantic and Pacific Tea Company. (An A & P oxcart stopped regularly at the farm in those days.) The Christmas party was still a glory in 1940 — but it was not as memorable as it was to my mother. Now people gave each other presents at home. Now the radio told us stories; now motorcars sped us to church. In Connecticut on Sunday nights my mother made sandwiches, crusts cut off, while we sat in a little circle around the radio to laugh together at Jack Benny and Fred Allen. Here, at my first church Christmas party, I felt conscious of my separateness — sophisticated visitor from the suburbs, sitting in a hard pew hearing six country girls and three boys stand and tell the birth story in words from the Gospels. Martha played the flute, Edna sang "It Was the Cold Midwinter" a cappella, Willard recited "'Twas the Night Before Christmas," and a three-year-old got halfway through a four-line poem. Gradually the country rituals, partly old and partly new, took me over. I forgot who I was and where I was as I joined the church-party world. I clasped my grandfather's hand. With his other hand he fed me the same wintergreen peppermint candies — in the same pew, in the same church — he gave me all summer, every Sunday, to distract me.

When the Sunday school pupils finished their individual performances, they trooped together to the back of the church while the congregation sang "Silent Night." We turned to see them bunched together at the back, costumed to begin the pageant. An older girl, haloed in cardboard over her blue dress, walked down the aisle to become Mary, followed by a younger Joseph, dressed in a cut-down bathrobe and grinning when he should have been solemn. Two angels with cardboard wings walked behind them, then shepherds with crooks and wise men with paper crowns. They gathered around the cradle as Mary embraced the doll Jesus. Some seemed dumbstruck, others giggled as they spoke their immemorial lines.

My grandmother pumped the organ again, "O Little Town of Bethlehem," while the children trooped to the back of the church, shedding their costumes. Uncle Luther labored up the platform, and we dropped our eyes for a final prayer. The Christmas program was over, and Mrs. Sanborn thanked the performers, who brought out a blooming poinsettia. It thrilled her, as if she did not receive a poinsettia every year. In turn, she gave each of the children, in folded red tissue paper, a Milky Way bar like the ones for sale in Ordway's store, across the road by the South Danbury depot called Converse.

· · ·

After the church's children finished off the popcorn balls, Caroline drove us home. We lit our tree, turned off while we were gone lest a hot bulb set fire to drying needles. My grandfather stoked the stoves and added fresh logs. We tuned in Gabriel Heatter, orotund and dramatic, talking about the gallant young lads of the RAF. Caroline cut slices from a mince pie she had cooked in Massachusetts, which we ate with gusto. Gram drank her Moxie and Gramp ate a diminished bread and milk. Gram filled our hot-water bottles, screwing the tops tight. When we went to bed, I heard, as ever, my grandparents praying, their soft and separate voices braided together.

TUESDAY

W E WOKE ON THE MORNING of Christmas Eve. I felt my time growing short, for I would leave the day after Christmas. I climbed with my grandfather to the tie-up again. This time when I sat on the three-legged stool he recited "Casey at the Bat," probably the most exalted literature in his repertoire. However, he never spoke the original poem. He recited a version where Casey hit a home run instead of striking out. Gramp could never stand it that the mighty Casey struck out. Soon, my grandfather with his ax climbed Ragged again, but without his lunch pail, because it would be a short workday. He came down from the hill at noon, heavily muffled and carrying his ax. He leaned low over the range, warming up, and we had our midday dinner. After we ate, Gramp and I crossed the road toward the henhouse. Gramp carried a hatchet and leaned it against a small chopping block. I watched as he entered the chicken coop, stepped past the haughty rooster, past three chickens gobbling leftovers, into a part of the structure where young hens sat roosting. There was a moment of squawking, and he emerged carrying two white birds upside down. Each hand held a pair of yellow legs, wings spread out on either side. Tomorrow these chickens would become our Christmas dinner, when more family would gather with us.

Our breaths blew white in the cold as my grandfather handed me one hen to hold by the feet. "Here, boy." I was nervous, never having held an upside-down chicken before. Gramp carried his hen to the chopping block, lay her head down, and with one blow of his hatchet cut it off. I had watched in the summer as chickens without heads ran furiously around the yard. This afternoon in the snow, the clattering hen would have squawked if she had anything left to squawk with, and raced in circles for what seemed to be minutes before she fell over without twitching, admitting that she was dead. In school I had read about the French Revolution. Was Robespierre conscious for a moment after the guillotine? My grandfather smiled at the dead fury; I laughed. For people who grow up on a farm, these things aren't overly unsettling.

Gramp killed the second hen and carried the carcasses to the kitchen, where the hard work began. My grandmother, her arms bare to the elbows, began to prepare the main course for tomorrow's Christmas dinner. She plucked a mound of white feathers, which would one day plump up a bed or a new pillow, and eviscerated the hens. Caroline chopped inner organs for the stuffing. Within the hens' uterine passages, we saw a series of eggs, tiny to large, which when matured would have plopped down into straw nests. A heap of hen remainders collected in a bowl to be scattered in the coop for unwitting chicken cannibals. As Gram cleaned out the carcasses, Caroline continued to assemble the stuffing, crumbling stale bread and chopped innards together, adding pepper and salt, vinegar and apple cider, neither too sweet nor too sour, setting her ingredients to simmer together at the back of the stove. Then she gathered ingredients for tomorrow's gravy. I offered to help, but there wasn't much I could do.

It was late in the darkening afternoon by the time everything was prepared for dinner, everything that could be done the day before. We still had an hour before supper. Caroline drove me to Henry's store, also the West Andover post office, half a mile down the road toward Gale. Henry Powers was everything: postmaster as well as storekeeper, with a hand-operated gasoline pump in front of the store to complete his facilities. The grocery lacked refrigeration but carried coffee, salt, and the toilet paper that replaced the Sears catalogue when the bathroom replaced the outhouse. There were cans of Spam, there were candy bars. Caroline and I brought Henry a dozen eggs, which we traded for two rolls of Scott tissue. Henry entered the cubicle that was the post office, and we picked up postcards addressed to Kate and Wesley Wells. In summers I hiked to Henry's place every morning for the mail and to pick up any groceries we needed, sauntering idly along the gutter of Route 4, passing the farms each with a few cows, one old farmer, and a big garden, passing the boulder that Riley shied at. Most of the year my grandfather walked down every day with three postcards, in 1940 still a penny, with Ben Franklin's face where a stamp would be. Every day Gram wrote a postcard to each of her daughters, and every day she had three

postcards back. Her eldest daughter was in a Connecticut hospital, but that did not keep her from writing a bulletin to her mother: She felt better. Donnie must be there now. There were snow flurries in Connecticut. Maybe there'd be a white Christmas? From Boston Nan wrote that she'd picked up Donnie at South Station. The bookstore was busy. Dick would be on leave Christmas Day. Caroline wrote that she was on her way.

Just past Henry's store was the house where he and Nettie lived, and across the street their daughter Nina and her husband Charlie. My mother remembered West Andover in her childhood as a crowded village, which now had mostly vanished. A cellar hole beyond Henry's had been the Daniel Webster Inn (Daniel Webster drank whiskey there), where drummers used to stay overnight, and across the road another cellar hole had belonged to a grocery store five times bigger than Henry's. My mother's West Andover also comprised a butcher, a fishmonger, and a livery stable, where drummers rented horses to sell their wares in the hills and hamlets. In a world transformed by the automobile, my mother's village had become only its depot and Henry Powers's place.

Our return took Gram away from opening Ball jars, up

from the cellar, for tomorrow's vegetables. She sat by the set tub in a rocking chair under Christopher the canary and read the postcards from her girls. She wrote three of her own, although they wouldn't get to the P.O. until the day after Christmas, including one to Caroline, who stood beside her. (When Caroline drove home she would need to find a postcard waiting.) In Connecticut I sometimes read what Gram wrote my mother: Two feet of snow. Wesley hauling ice. Earlene has fat around the heart. How's Donnie's sniffles?

Caroline and Gram finished stuffing the uncooked hens and covered them with damp dishcloths and put them in kettles with lids on top and rocks on top of lids, to discourage mice. Christmas Eve supper was leftovers from Christmas Eve dinner. Before we drank Moxie and ate bread and milk, we put our last packages under the tree for the morning. Gabriel Heatter boomed and we went to bed.

WEDNESDAY

CHRISTMAS MORNING. As soon as we all awoke, dressed, and ate a quick breakfast, we sat in the living room gazing at the tree with its bright gathering of gifts underneath. The fire blazed in the kitchen range, where my grandmother had already started to cook the hens. The living room Glenwood warmed us. My grandfather had milked the cows while Caroline and I were sleeping, and now we sat to open our presents. I had brought a package that my parents had wrapped for Caroline. There were new brown bib overalls for my grandfather, and for my grandmother a warm woolen cardigan. My father had wrapped an oddly shaped package for me to give my grandparents. Gramp whooped when he opened it: a bunch of bananas! In New Hampshire, in 1940, nobody ate tropical fruit. Gramp in particular adored bananas, and he was lucky to eat one a year. Florida's oranges might be sold at Town Meeting, but you never saw the Mesoamerican banana.

For me there were the anticipated mittens knitted by my grandmother, to replace last year's, which I had been wearing thin and holey. Another of my packages was a scarf that Gram had knitted as well. I didn't get a scarf every year and immediately modeled it. Caroline gave me a collection of *The Best American Short Stories,* just published, which flattered and pleased me. I picked up another package, slim but heavy. My grandfather grinned, so I knew it came from him. It was an old book, *One Hundred and One Famous Poems,* tattered and with a birthday inscription dated 1912, names unfamiliar. "The McHarveys had a yard sale," said Gramp, "and I was walking by . . ." Everybody knew that in summers I tried writing poems each morning while my grandfather and Riley mowed hay. The book began with Longfellow, his white-bearded face engraved above "The Builders" ("All architects of Fate / . . . with massive deeds and great") and ending one hundred poems later with Rudyard Kipling's

"L'Envoy" ("When earth's last picture is painted, and the tales are twisted and dried, / When the oldest colors have faded, and the youngest critic has died"). Poetry ended, but not the book: A "Prose Supplement" began with the Gettysburg Address, then the Ten Commandments, the Magna Carta, Patrick Henry's "Give me liberty or give me death," and the Declaration of Independence. I looked through the poetry and exclaimed, again and again, while Gramp continued to grin.

The hens were cooking in the range's oven, with vegetables in pots spread over the top of the stove, emptied jars on the set tubs. From the garden there were peas, string beans, corn niblets, potatoes, squash, and onions. Pumpkin and apple pies lay underneath the kitchen clock that Gramp wound every night before bed. Gram played the oven as she played the organ, only with greater skill. Regularly she checked a thermometer and adjusted heat by turning a handle on the stovepipe or opening a draft underneath the firebox. She shuttled from the oven to the pots of vegetables, lifting a lid, reaching for a mitt. I helped by bringing more wood from the woodshed. Caroline bustled to make pots of coffee and move saucepans from hotter to cooler places on the stove. Because company was coming, Caroline and I pulled the dining room table apart, adding a width of tabletop. We spread out my grandmother's cherished lace tablecloth and set seven places — for my grandparents, for Caroline, for Uncle Luther, for me, and for another couple, my grandfather's sister Aunt Lottie and her husband Uncle Gene Currier.

Gramp grew up at his father's blacksmith shop on a hill overlooking South Danbury. He was born in 1875, a decade after his father came home from the Civil War. By 1940 most of his siblings had died or moved away, but his sister Lottie lived nearby with Gene Currier, who was a chicken farmer. They drove a Ford and could easily travel the five miles from their farm to ours. Often we visited them in summer, and toured their sheds of Rhode Island Reds, which produced dozens and dozens of eggs they loaded once a week onto a Boston truck. A dinner of poultry was the last thing they needed; that's why we cooked young chickens instead of old hens. Anyway, they liked to be with family at Christmas.

Before they came, Caroline picked up Uncle Lu, doubtless to prevent any adventures with his Studebaker, and when she rolled with him into the yard before noon, Lottie and Gene had just arrived. We gathered in the driveway for the welcoming, some of us warmly dressed and the rest freezing. Gene and Gramp pulled apart from the rest of us for a moment. I knew that my grandfather rarely talked with another grown man, and I knew something else too, from my summer visits. Gene was speaking into Gramp's ear, and I heard Gramp's secret laugh. Gene told jokes or stories that only my grandfather was to hear. Once in the summer Gene spoke a word or two that, from Gramp's quick look at me, I knew I was not supposed to hear. In my grandmother's house, both "gosh" and "darn" were devilish obscenities.

We went inside to the living room, two on the small sofa, Luther in a Morris chair made of wood and leather, two in regular chairs, two in green kitchen chairs added for the crowd. We paid special attention to the Curriers, who hadn't been at the farm since last spring. I heard Lottie say, "Pullets turned into the best hens we've ever had. Lay day and night."

"No trouble with critters?" Gramp asked.

"There's a fox hangs around," said Gene. "I keep my shotgun loaded."

Lottie smiled and added, "Last summer Gene trapped six skunks." Gene pinched his nose.

Caroline and Gram moved off to the kitchen, followed by Gramp. It was nearly noon and everyone expected to start eating no later. In the living room Luther was talking to Gene and Lottie about how his family raised poultry when he was a boy. It was trains that took eggs to Boston then, but you had to watch out for Boston's count — those egg people kept claiming breakage. Luther remembered his father Benjamin's trip to Boston to investigate, and when he went, he . . .

"Same with the trucks now," said Gene, "but you don't know, damn it . . ." Luther pretended not to hear the blasphemy.

From the kitchen came sounds of dinner assembling. Caroline brought glasses of sweet water to the table, hand-pumped from the well beside the toolshed. (Our faucet water, coming downhill from the mountain, sometimes contained a bit of mountain.) In the kitchen the bustle included Gramp slicing the hens, muttering from time to time. I saw Gram and Caroline empty boiling water from pots into colanders, then carry full dishes of potatoes and peas and onions to the dining room table. Caroline brought in the plate of stuffing, and my grandfather followed with a huge china serving dish, which I had never seen before, piled with cut slices of dark meat and white, beside legs and wings.

Called to the table, we found it covered with food from end to end: chicken and stuffing, vegetables, mashed potatoes, gravy, butter, vinegar in a cruet. Uncle Luther presided at the far end of the table, Gramp at the near end by the plate stacked with chicken. Lottie and Gene sat on one side, Gram and Caroline and I across. First thing, Luther closed his eyes and said grace. "Dear Lord, we thank Thee . . ." He went on and on while the smell of food made us hungry. Finally, my grandfather distributed the chicken, plate by plate, asking for preferences. Three legs went quickly, leaving one for Gramp, who served himself last. Next to each portion of meat huddled a spoonful of stuffing, and as the plates rounded the table, so did bowls of vegetables and the gravy boat. Everything on the table, except for salt and pepper, came from the acres of Eagle Pond Farm.

Uncle Luther started eating before anyone else. As we were deep into dinner, the phone rang. "It's for you, Donnie." I had been expecting it. My mother told me that she was *much* better, but she still sounded weak. She was in bed at home — in Connecticut we had *two* telephones, one beside the double bed — and she was sorry to call right while we were eating but she knew we would all be there by now. She asked about my presents, and I spoke of *One Hundred and One Famous Poems*. I said that Gramp and Gram loved the bananas.

The telephone was still a frightening object for the older people. It hung on the wall in the dining room, a brown wooden box with a mouthpiece sticking out on top. From a cord dangled the receiver which you put to your ear. On the side was a handle to turn when you wanted to make a call. Everybody living in the country had a party line, and reached their neighbors by turning the handle the right number of times. If you called any distance, like Andover or Connecticut, you cranked once, said, "Hello, Central," and told Central what you wanted. Long distance was expensive, and conversations were quick. After I talked with my mother, everyone stood in line to say "Merry Christmas," holding the earphone as if it might assault them. No one but Caroline (and I suppose Donnie) talked in a natural voice. Gram sounded like one of her postcards, only hesitant. Lottie spoke more easily than Gene, who barked for six seconds. My grandfather was most nervous of all. He addressed the speaker, as far away as the ear cord would allow him, in a high voice of terror. I ended the call by talking again with my parents, about tomorrow when the train would bring me late to New Haven. We'd have *our* Christmas when Mom felt stronger. As I hung up, I felt melancholy about leaving this table, Gramp and Gram and Eagle Pond Farm.

All of us went back to cleaning our plates and babbled about the miracle of talking all the way to Connecticut. Everything had changed so much in the lives of the older people. Even Caroline joined in, who remembered the time of kerosene lamps, before the farm afforded electric lights or a telephone, before neighbors began to replace horses with automobiles. Gramp spoke of airplanes. One with pontoons had landed on Eagle Pond! Now folks were flying across the ocean, more recently because of the war. "For my father," said Gram, "it was the same with trains. My goodness, he was twenty-two years old before the railroad tracks came to Potter Place and Gale. He lived long enough to take a train all the way to Boston. Twice."

"Last Monday," said Gene, "I waited ten minutes at the crossing in Andover while a freight train went by. Two locomotives. Must have been a hundred cars."

"Going north?" asked Gramp.

"You said there was airplanes," Lottie said to Gene.

"Fuselage on one car, wings on another," said Gene. "Headed for Montreal, King Franklin the First sending war stuff to England." Uncle Gene's politics did not resemble my grandfather's. Gramp did not rise to the bait: it was Christmas.

"One day it'll be soldiers," said Caroline mournfully.

Uncle Luther looked up from his plate. "When I was nine," he said, "I watched the soldier boys walking home from Virginia."

"One was my father," said Gramp.

Soon all of us had finished our plates, some after second helpings. Lottie, Gram, and Caroline took them into the kitchen, scraping and rinsing. Uncle Luther picked at his teeth, although they were false. (Everybody but Caroline and I had false teeth.) We talked about the war in Europe: Nazis overrunning France, Dunkirk, FDR Lend-Leasing fifty old destroyers to England. We spoke of the first peacetime draft in the United States. I croaked off-tune the lines of a new song: "Good-bye dear, I'll be back in a year / 'cause I'm in the army now." Gene muttered, Uncle Lu sighed, Gramp spoke oratorically about Roosevelt, Gene muttered again.

Caroline returned from the kitchen with her hands full of smaller plates, and Lottie followed with a custard pie she had baked. Gram brought an apple pie in one hand, pumpkin in the other. I ate pieces of all three. Uncle Luther needed the bathroom, which had been installed in 1938 just off the dining room. Everyone talked louder in order not to listen. (People under eighty, when the dining room was occupied, walked through the toolshed to the semiretired five-hole outhouse.) When we finished eating pie we pushed back our chairs to accommodate our bellies. Gramp offered slices of banana, but we said we were too full. The women cleared the table again. This time I thought to help out, then joined the men in the living room while the kitchen crew washed, dried, and restored the china to the pantry.

We stretched our legs and talked about old times, especially about the people we missed, 1940's losses. Telling these stories was collective mourning — regret, affection, and amusement all together. The women joined us from the kitchen, overhearing our talk. "I do miss Free," said Gram. Freeman Morrison had been her cousin and childhood companion. We told each other Freeman stories, most of which we knew already. Everyone had always talked about Freeman as if he existed for the anecdotes he provided. When I first encountered him, he was a little old man who lived alone in a shack on the side of Ragged Mountain. Sometimes he walked down the dirt road five miles to Eagle Pond Farm and his cousin Kate, who had a room ready for him. "Freeman's room" was upstairs across from the Best Room. In his bedroom he kept his collection of wall clocks, and hung up a 1929 calendar beside a dangling wasp's nest. There was a black chest, like a pirate's chest, crammed with diaries and clippings from magazines. When he felt sick, or when he wanted to talk to people rather than to his ox, he visited and stayed in his room. It had a chair but no bed, and neither did his shack, where Freeman slept sitting up in a broken Morris chair, its missing leg replaced by Montgomery Ward catalogues. Six months ago, when I was haying with my grandfather, Freeman's legs were giving out, and he slept next to our kitchen range in a rocking chair with rollers so flat it could not rock. As always, he talked without stopping, an endless autobiography about moving granite boulders, splicing branches onto apple trees, peddling Quaker Oil and Rawleigh's Salve from door to door, roofing a house by night with lanterns hanging from tree branches. After supper my grandparents and I sat in the living room while Free rambled on from the kitchen, making sense but never stopping. My grandmother tatted, and every now and then said, "Ay-yuh," just to let him know we were listening.

There was another eccentricity of Freeman's that I knew from early on. One summer on the farm when I was little, I watched my grandmother clean the pantry, emptying a small chest, turning over a drawer to shake out the mouse droppings. On the bottom of the drawer, where no one could see, firm black letters spelled out FREEMAN MORRISON, so big they seemed to shout his name. Gram told me, "You'll see Freeman's name everywhere, places it's hard to see. We never knew what he meant by it." She showed me where he had painted his name on the underside of a windowsill. Later I found it all over the house. In his room upstairs I must have found FREEMAN MORRISON half a dozen times — on the bottoms of shelves, under his black chest, on the back of the 1929 calendar.

Freeman, who was seven or eight years older than Kate, had moved to Eagle Pond Farm in the 1880s. His family farm had burned down, house and barn. Young Freeman and his brothers and sisters were each deposited with relatives. It was Freeman's good luck to be boarded with the Kenestons, Gram's parents. We knew that Freeman's cruel father had punished him routinely, savagely, and arbitrarily. Uncle Lu repeated aloud a story all of us remembered. One Christmas, when Freeman was ten years old, a cousin gave

him a pair of battered ice skates, the kind with clamps to
fasten on your boots. Freeman had always wanted skates but
his family had no money. He was happier with his cousin's
present than he had ever been in his life. He was too happy
to sleep that night, and the morning after Christmas missed
his five A.M. chores. To show him how bad he was, and to
make sure that he never overslept again, his father took
Freeman and his skates out to the middle of frozen Eagle
Pond, hacked a hole in the ice, and dropped the skates into
deep water.

For a while no one spoke. Then my grandmother told
about Freeman building her a playhouse when she was a
little girl, where she pretended to cook and clean. A generation later, middle-aged Freeman repaired it and put on a new
roof when Lucy, Caroline, and Nan were old enough to play
house. Caroline remembered Freeman creeping up when she
and her sisters were making imaginary pies, leaping from a
bush to scare them. Then Caroline told us something none
of us knew. "Once I snooped around in Freeman's room,"
she said. "Free was off somewhere, and I was visiting during vacation. When I opened his trunk, I learned that Free
was sweet on Mama. In the trunk he kept his diaries, going
back to 1889 or so, mostly telling the weather or what he'd

done—'Hayed two acres today'—but also I found a letter in there, not Free's handwriting, and it was from a woman he didn't know." None of us had ever heard anything of Freeman and a woman. "At the start she was indignant. I forget her name. 'How could a man write a strange woman such a letter!' she said. 'I am a respectable woman,' that sort of thing, but by the end of the letter she was talking like a coquette, flirting with this man she had never met. She sounded crazy. I figured that Free had read some lonelyhearts letter in a magazine—maybe a farm monthly—and was thinking about taking a wife. Then I saw the date on the letter, 1903. Mama and Poppa were married in 1903, and Free was looking for a wife, any wife, because Katie got married."

Gram looked pleased and said no, it couldn't be. My grandfather giggled. Then Luther spoke up suddenly, pointing out the window. "It's snowing. Look at it snow." The air was heavy with fine snowflakes, the kind that fall at the start of a big storm. It had already dropped two inches on the driveway, and you could hardly see the barn through the dense flakes. For a second I thought that maybe I wouldn't have to go home tomorrow . . . and then I remembered my sick mother and how she'd feel if I couldn't. Aunt Lottie said, "We'd better leave pretty soon." There was only one snowplow in town, an old truck fitted out, and there were lots of families on the back roads. Even on Route 4, the plow didn't clear the road clean until a day after the storm.

"Do you want to head back, Lu?" said Caroline.

"Pretty soon, I guess."

Then Uncle Gene said, "We can wait while I tell one more Freeman story." We nodded. "You might remember, Kate, you were still in high school, I suppose, Lottie and I bought the old house, starting out, and farmed with five cows, only a few chickens at first, and our roof leaked. We heard about Free and his shingling, I suppose from your father. Freeman was still young, but he was already the way he was. Mostly. He came over for a week or two, and roofed our house. He slept at night then, on a cot not a chair, up in an attic you climbed to on a ladder. He spent the daylight shingling, then after supper took long walks up the hills by himself. It was March, I think, muddy, but when he'd come back his boots had snow on them because he walked so high up-mountain. One night Lottie and I went to bed before he got back, and in the morning — he always slept late, even then, seven o'clock sometimes — we saw in the yard what he'd brought back the night before. It was a sled, and it looked almost new, with shiny runners and new wood planks, modern and fancy, not like the ones we clobbered together with shaved boards. This one had iron runners and looked like something out of a mail-order catalogue. Nobody had any notion of how it got left up-mountain."

Out the window we saw the snow that kept on falling, tiny and thick, covering the tops of the cars outside.

"Well, that day Freeman didn't do any roofing. First he sat out in the yard, cleaning and polishing his sled, though it looked cleaned and polished enough when we first laid eyes on it. In the middle of the morning Free took it back up the mountain — the hill, we used to call it. It was almost time for sugaring, but if you went up high, it was still winter and there was snow. Free sledded all day, finding places where he could dodge around trees, where it was straightaway, and the next day he did the same thing. We wondered when he'd get back to shingling. Those shingles, I remember, came from a mill over to Salisbury. Then it rained, turned warm, and I suppose Free helped us out around the farm until he could get back to roofing. Every night after supper he couldn't stop talking, talking, talking about sliding downhill. You know Free. After only two days of that sled, he was full of it — how he did this and that, tricks he learned and problems he thought about, ways to fix

63

them. I thought of that story about his father."

"Free found his skates again," said Caroline.

Nobody said anything. All of us were thinking of Freeman. And we thought about snow. I wondered how we'd manage to get to Gale for the morning Peanut, and there wasn't another passenger train for Boston until midday. Gene went on, "Well, that's almost the whole story, but there's one more thing. After Free moved out of the attic, Lottie and I didn't have any reason to climb that rickety ladder. It must have been two years. One day Lottie went looking for something she missed, which she couldn't find anywhere, and climbed up there. Beside the old cot she saw something big and long, covered with brown sheets of newspaper, little stones holding the newspaper from curling up. I followed her up the ladder to see what she found, when I got back from chores. Underneath the paper was the sled, still shining, right where Free left it — why didn't he come back for it? — and in the middle of the top he had written his own name, in big letters that went all the way from end to end."

When Uncle Gene finished, we murmured, shaking our heads. I thought of Freeman so young, so strange, so happy in Gene's story, and already writing FREEMAN MOR-RISON.

Then everyone stood up and looked out at the snow as it thickened in the yard. "Might be quite a winter," said my grandfather.

"Seems like August when it started," Gram said, "then only a few inches now and then, but it looks like a blizzard now. I remember the blizzard of '88. I was ten years old."

"Town Meeting day," said Gramp. "The only Town Meeting my father ever missed."

Luther looked pensive. "When I was a boy," he said, "they still talked about 1816. They called it the Poverty Year, with a freeze every single month, even July and August. People ate their seed potatoes. They boiled the corn they'd saved for seed."

"A volcano erupted two years before, half the world away," Caroline said. "I read about it. People thought it was God's punishment."

"It was," said Luther.

Uncle Lu put on his galoshes and Caroline held his arm as he shuffled to her car. She took a minute to clear off her windshield; no need to scrape because the snow was so dry. The Curriers did the same, and the two cars drove out onto Route 4, Gene and Lottie turning left toward Andover,

Caroline right toward Uncle Luther's Sabine. He wanted to spend the night in his little house, snow or no snow. When she returned, she said she was glad she didn't have to drive any farther. A little later, my grandmother rang up Central for the Curriers. They'd gotten home all right. Lottie said that Gene was out with the chickens, shutting them in from the snow.

Gramp had already changed out of his brown suit into his overalls and sweaters and coats and boots. He climbed slowly to the barn, and I tagged after him. Cows needed milking, Christmas Day or not. He spoke "'Twas the Night Before Christmas," even though we had heard it at church two nights before. He spoke it better than the boy at church. Riley needed water and a ration of oats, the chickens and sheep their feed. When we came back, we shook off snow in the toolshed and went into the kitchen. Gramp's face was red and his chest heaving. He was happy.

Supper stripped the hens clean and finished the vegetables. Gram and Caroline filled a pot with water, dumped in the chicken bones, and set it on the stove. The water on top would freeze that night, but in the morning they would boil the bones to make soup. Tonight we were tired, and we knew that when we got up we would be busy. We never tuned in

Gabriel Heatter. Before bed I walked out on the porch to see how high the snow was. It was too dark to tell. Then I saw the headlights of the Boston and Maine's railroad plow, a swooping metal blade pushed by a single locomotive. The trains ran on time. But if the snow kept on, how would we get to Gale in a buggy with wheels that were lower than the snowdrifts? Back inside, I asked my grandfather, "Can we get to the Peanut?"

"We'll see," he said. "Yes."

It took me longer than usual to go to sleep that night. I wanted to get to Connecticut and my mother. I wanted to stay at Eagle Pond Farm all winter.

THURSDAY

THE PEANUT WAS DUE at Gale at seven forty-five A.M. I heard my grandparents get up. Kerosene exploded in the kitchen range, then in the living room Glenwood. Coffee snorted in the percolator. My bedroom windows were frosted over and I needed to see how deep the snow was, so I climbed out of bed and quickly pulled on my clothes. My grandmother poured a cup of coffee. "Your Gramp's still in the tie-up," she told me. In the twilight before sunrise, I looked out the window at his tracks, big holes for his boots and shallow trenches made by his knees. I turned to look at the road but I couldn't see it. "Town plow went by," said Gram as she braided her hair. I strained to look, and saw a depression in the middle of Route 4. Then I looked across the yard at the buggy shed under the barn. Snow had drifted into it, past the front wheels of the buggy, and the drifts looked three feet high. "Gram, should we call my folks?"

"Gramp says he thinks you'll go," Gram said. "I wish you could stay, but Lucy needs you. Are you packed?"

I wasn't. I went back to my bedroom and packed. I hadn't brought much, so it was easy. The new mittens and the scarf fit into my suitcase, and my books. I ate breakfast. Gram had warmed up brown bread left from our first supper, and on the table were yesterday's leftover pies. Caroline, shaggy with sleep and wearing a pink bathrobe with pink slippers, sat beside me and ate a slice of her Massachusetts mince. She was staying on, before going back to her school. (I knew she had a date for New Year's Eve.) When I stood up from the table, an hour before my train was supposed to go, my grandmother insisted that I put on my winter coat and sit beside my suitcase in the kitchen by the door. I wasn't surprised.

I waited, looking up at the barn to see if my grandfather would open one of the doors and lead Riley in harness toward the carriage. Not yet. It was almost seven o'clock. Then I saw the two big doors slide open on their rollers, the barn as wide open as it was when we drove the summer hayrack in. Riley trotted out pulling the sleigh that had not been used for fifteen years, Gramp sitting on the curved seat, holding the reins and grinning from ear to ear. Beside me, Gram and Caroline clapped their hands together. "Surprise!" said Caroline.

We hugged each other saying goodbye. I bundled out the door with my suitcase, snow above my knees, and climbed into the sleigh beside my grandfather. The cobwebs were gone, and Riley high-stepped — as if he remembered from fifteen years ago — while we turned onto Route 4, our runners spraying white showers beside us.

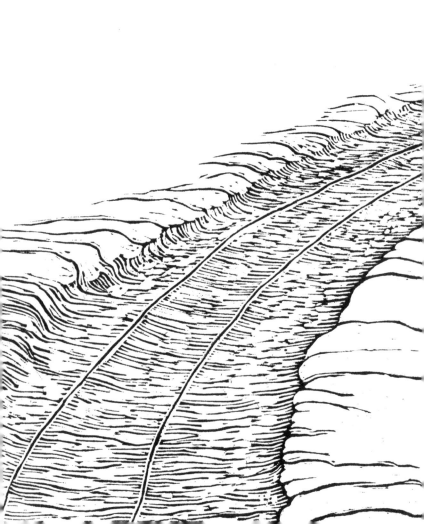

I did not go to Eagle Pond at Christmas in 1940. In summers when I was a boy I took the train to my grandparents' farm, haying with my grandfather and hearing his thousand stories. During the school year in Connecticut, I read the postcards my grandmother wrote: autumn leaves, Christmas, the first daffodils. My mother told me stories about winter at Eagle Pond Farm, where my grandfather chopped timber and hauled ice, and about the Christmas parties at church. I wanted desperately to visit for Christmas, but it never worked out. From my summer visits I knew all the people in this book. I remember how they talked.

The only survivor of old times, I moved here for good in 1975. In my eighties I inhabit the beloved place, mourning and celebrating the golden dead, as bright as Freeman's discovery in the hills. In this book, I have given myself the thing I most wanted, a boyhood Christmas at Eagle Pond Farm.

A NOTE ON THE TYPE

Christmas on Eagle Pond is set in ITC Founder's Caslon 12, a revival by the late Justin Howes (1963–2005). Howes utilized the vast resources of the St Bride Printing Library in London to study the types of William Caslon I, and developed this text-size face from the 12-point specimens in the Library's archives. Released in 1998, it is a faithful revival of Caslon's type, and meant to be used specifically at text size. Howes also issued a 42-point cut for display use. Caslon's types were the product of the 17th century. The matrices from which the types were cast were struck from hand-cut punches. As a result, every character in each size of Caslon's types was different. Howes honored those differences in his decision to model text and display sizes on those specific specimens found at St Brides.

MJB